Lerner SPORTS

EXTREME SPEED

SUPERFAST FORMULA 1 RACING

Dustin Albino

Lerner Publications ◆ Minneapolis

CONTENTS

CHAPTER 1

FORMULA 1 ON THE RISE

Bottas (front) zoomed around turns at the Chinese Grand Prix.

All eyes at the Shanghai International Circuit in Shanghai, China, were on Lewis Hamilton and Valtteri Bottas. The Mercedes teammates pulled into the pit lane on lap 36 of the 2019 Chinese **Grand Prix**. Hamilton led from the start of the race, pulling ahead of the other **open-wheel** cars on the cold, wet track. Bottas had been close behind. This pit stop was a risk for Mercedes. Would the "Silver Arrows" lose their lead? Could Ferrari drivers Sebastian Vettel and Charles Leclerc overcome them to win the day?

FACTS AT A GLANCE

- More than four million fans attended at least one Formula 1 race in 2018.

- Each pit crew has up to 20 members.

- A Formula 1 steering wheel has an overtake button, also known as "push-to-pass," that helps drivers speed up to get ahead of other cars.

- The Monaco Grand Prix is one of the most famous Formula 1 races each year. It takes place on the city streets of Monte Carlo.

Hamilton, still in first, pulled out of the pit lane, zoomed around the course's hairpin turns, and picked up speed on the straightaway. Bottas emerged in third place behind Leclerc, but Leclerc didn't stand a chance against Bottas's new tires. Leclerc could not keep up and fell into fifth place. Not even a last-minute pit and new tires could help him catch up. The Mercedes risk paid off. Hamilton and Bottas came in first and second place.

Hamilton posed for photos after winning the 2019 Chinese Grand Prix.

The high speeds during a Formula 1 race make it an exciting sport to watch.

This is the world of Formula 1 racing. More than four million fans attended at least one Formula 1 race in 2018. On average, almost 195,000 fans came out on a given weekend. Spectators love Formula 1 because of the extreme speeds that cars can achieve. During a grand prix, cars can reach speeds of almost 230 miles (370 km) per hour.

The 2019 Chinese Grand Prix marked the 1,000th Formula 1 race in the history of the world championship series. Nino Farina won the first world championship series in 1950. Driver Michael Schumacher holds the record for winning the most championships. He claimed the title seven times between 1994 and 2004. Today's drivers, such as Hamilton and Vettel, seek to make their own mark in the Formula 1 history books.

Formula 1 has undergone plenty of changes over the course of 1,000 races. The car's engine type and body shape have been modified, and safety has become a priority for the sport. But one thing has remained constant: the thrill of the race.

Fans of Sebastian Vettel showed their support at the 2019 Chinese Grand Prix.

CHAPTER 2
THE FORMULA 1 CAR

Though each Formula 1 car has a slightly different design, all cars must adhere to strict guidelines in order to compete.

are often displayed on the car.

As technology improves, Formula 1 cars become faster, safer, and more durable. Teams create cars that cost millions of dollars. Team Mercedes had a budget of approximately $450 million during the 2016 race season. Large teams have more money to spend on high-quality parts and racers. All teams have to adhere to the same formula, or guidelines, when building their vehicles. Even the tiniest difference can lead to an unfair advantage.

Building a Formula 1 car starts with the chassis. The chassis is the main part of the race car to which all other parts are attached. It is built from lightweight metal. It is strong enough to withstand the high speeds and forces of race day.

Each chassis has an open cockpit where the driver sits. Every driver has a custom seat. This helps keep them safe and comfortable on the road.

REALLY?!

As of 2018, even the weight of the driver was considered when changing rules for Formula 1 racing. Drivers must weigh at least 176 pounds (80 kg) and cars must weigh at least 1,455 pounds (660 kg). Lighter cars can travel faster. A minimum weight limit makes sure that heavier drivers are not at a disadvantage.

Every part of a Formula 1 car
is designed to maximize speed.

Formula 1 cars are designed to be as **aerodynamic** as
possible. Cars must create a lot of downward force while also
reducing **drag**. Formula 1 cars are wide and sit low to the
ground. Every Formula 1 car has a front **wing** and a rear wing
that direct airflow. **Endplates** on each side of the front wing
move air around the front tires, which reduces air resistance.
The wing also increases the downward force, which helps the
car stay on the track around tight turns.

Formula 1 tires maximize speed too. The front tires must be between 12 and 15 inches (30 and 38 cm) wide, and the rear tires must be between 14 and 15 inches (36 and 38 cm) wide. The tires are very soft, which helps them grip the track and increases the speed of the car. However, these soft tires do not last very long. Drivers must make frequent pit stops to replace their tires.

Different Formula 1 tires have different levels of softness. This changes how the tires grip the track under different road conditions.

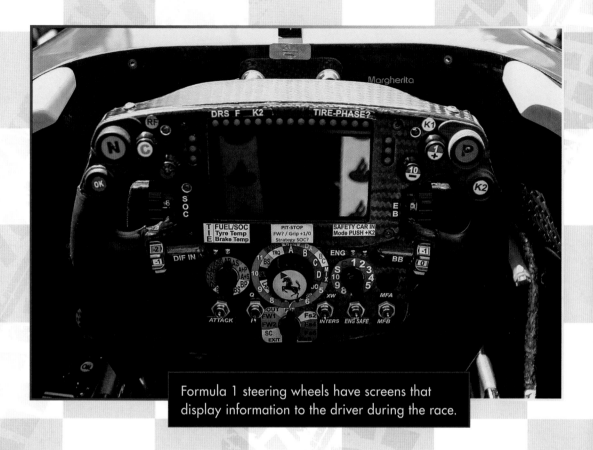

Formula 1 steering wheels have screens that display information to the driver during the race.

A Formula 1 steering wheel is small and has dozens of buttons. Each button controls a different aspect of the car. The overtake button, also known as "push-to-pass," helps drivers speed up to get ahead of other cars. Another button activates the Drag Reduction System (DRS). Each race track has at least one DRS activation zone. Pushing the DRS button moves a rear wing on the car, which reduces drag and provides more speed.

CHAPTER 3

INSIDE KNOWLEDGE

Many people work together to prepare racers for the grand prix.

Formula 1 racers still compete, even when it's raining.

Formula 1 races take place over an entire weekend. The grand prix is the final event on Sunday. Most teams arrive on Thursday to prepare for the race. Friday and Saturday feature practice sessions and qualifying races. These help drivers get to know the track and the race conditions. Racers can also make sure their cars are in good shape and have all of their safety features working. The qualifying race decides the starting order for the grand prix.

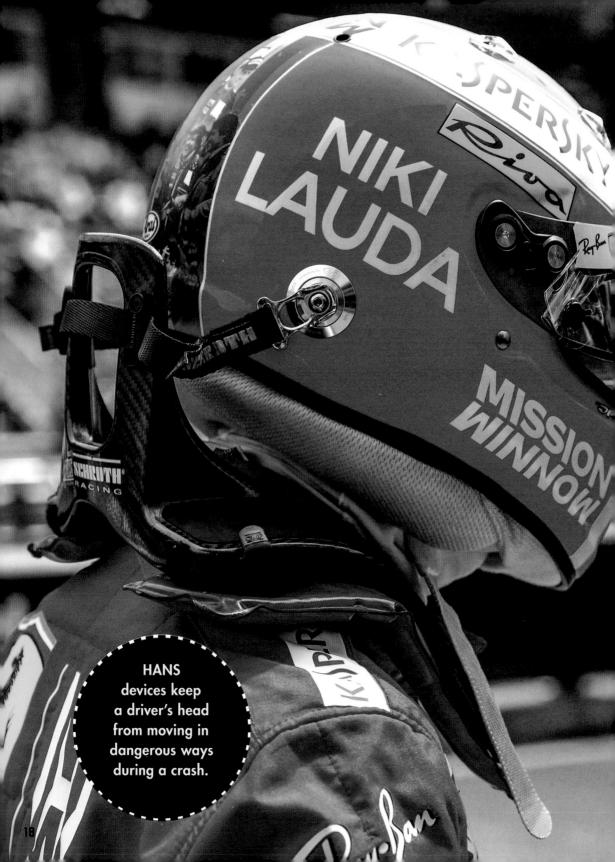

HANS devices keep a driver's head from moving in dangerous ways during a crash.

Formula 1 cars have many safety features to protect drivers. All drivers wear **HANS devices**, which provide support to their head and neck. They also wear fire suits in case the car catches on fire during a collision. Each car also has a circuit breaker that the driver can push to cut off all of the car's electrical circuits. This can help slow down a car and make it safer in a crash.

The pit crew practices before the race too. They time how quickly they can change tires, make adjustments, and refuel the car. Each crew has up to 20 members. They all have different jobs to do on race day.

REALLY?!

Formula 1 brakes are made from a material called carbon fiber. They are strong and lightweight. They also work in really high temperatures, up to 2,200 degrees Fahrenheit (1,200°C). This is important because Formula 1 brakes get very hot. Braking at high speeds creates a lot of energy and heat. The brakes can sometimes get so hot that they glow red.

Safety measures are also important to pit crews. Drivers can press a button on the steering wheel that imposes a speed limit on the car. The pit lane speed limit is approximately 50 miles (80 km) per hour. This protects the pit crew when cars enter and exit a pit stop.

Crew members wear fire suits to protect them while working.

Some drivers sign autographs for fans during race weekend.

Before a race, drivers and pit crew members give fans tours of the garages or cars. They also participate in press conferences or parties. They may even demonstrate new technology or features on the cars. But everyone is looking forward to seeing the cars in the grand prix.

Before each race, pit crews inspect all of the car's parts, such as the engine, wings, and tires.

Fans of driver Max Verstappen made a sign showing their support before the 2018 Austrian Grand Prix.

On race day, pit crews prepare final touches to the pit stop and garage. Drivers prepare too. They make sure they are rested, hydrated, and in peak physical condition for the race. Every second counts during the race itself.

Fans arrive early to watch events before the grand prix. They can buy merchandise and food. Many people get autographs with their favorite drivers. Fans can even watch other racing events or demonstrations. All of this builds excitement for the final race.

Cars have to navigate carefully around each other when trying to take over the lead position.

Drivers line up into the starting grid based on the positions they earned during qualifying races. The driver in first place is in **pole position**. All of the cars then take a formation lap, or parade lap, around the track. Then it's time for the race to begin. Once the drivers get the green light, the cars accelerate rapidly to battle for the title.

PROFILE IN
SPEED

NICO ROSBERG. Nico Rosberg won three consecutive races at Monaco between 2013 and 2015. The 2013 win was exactly 30 years after his father, Formula 1 driver Keke Rosberg, won the Monaco Grand Prix. During his career, Nico Rosberg won 23 grand prixs, as well as the 2016 Formula 1 World Championship.

The Monaco Grand Prix takes place during the summer. People can watch the race from nearby hotels and apartment buildings.

Formula 1 races have different track lengths and types, so each race is different. The Monaco Grand Prix takes places on the city streets of Monte Carlo. The track is narrow, which makes it difficult for cars to overtake each other. It is also 78 laps long. The race in Monaco is one of the most famous races each year.

The final race of the season is at Yas Marina Circuit in Abu Dhabi, United Arab Emirates. It takes place on a closed track on an island. The island was built specifically for Formula 1 races. Many fans come to Formula 1 weekend at the circuit to celebrate the end of the racing season. There is even a concert once the race ends.

The Yas Marina Circuit track loops through two hotel buildings.

Visitors to the Geneva International Motor Show in Switzerland can view Formula 1 cars on display.

From the very first Formula 1 race to now, the sport has seen a lot of change. It continues to grow in popularity, gaining more and more fans in the United States each year. In the future, the engines, chassis, wings, and other features may change to provide even more speed. These changes would help make Formula 1 racing even more exciting for its devoted fans.

FORMULA 1
FAMILY TREE

Formula 1 cars have changed drastically over the years, but one thing has stayed the same—they're made to go fast!

Nino Farina, 1950s

Jochen Rindt, 1970s

Eddie Irvine, 1990s

Kevin Magnussen, 2010s

GLOSSARY

aerodynamic
having features that maximize airflow and increase speed

drag
air resistance as a car moves forward

endplates
vertical panels at the edge of the car's front wings

grand prix
the main event of a Formula 1 race weekend, where points are awarded to drivers toward the world championship

HANS device
short for Head and Neck Support device, a mandatory safety device that prevents excessive head and neck movement during an accident

open-wheel
a type of racing where the wheels are not covered, which causes air to hit the tires and increase speeds

pole position
the first place on the starting grid, awarded to the driver who had the fastest qualifying lap

wing
the front or rear piece of a Formula 1 car that helps reduce drag

FURTHER INFORMATION

Challen, Paul. *Formula 1 Racing*. New York: PowerKids Press, 2015.

Formula 1
https://www.formula1.com

Levit, Joe. *Auto Racing's G.O.A.T.* Minneapolis: Lerner Publications, 2019.

Racing Cars
https://www.dkfindout.com/uk/transport/history-cars/racing-cars

Silverman, Buffy. *How Do Formula One Race Cars Work?* Minneapolis: Lerner Publications, 2016.

Suen, Anastasia. *Auto Racers*. Vero Beach, FL: Rourke, 2019.

INDEX

PHOTO ACKNOWLEDGMENTS

The images in this book are used with the permission of: © motorsports Photographer/Shutterstock.com, pp. 4, 7, 8–9; © Kristin Greenwood/Shutterstock.com, pp. 5, 29 (bottom right); © Anadolu Agency/Getty Images, p. 6; © Shahjehan/Shutterstock.com, pp. 10, 20, 21; © Marco Canoniero/Shutterstock.com, p. 11; © cristiano barni/Shutterstock.com, pp. 13, 16, 26; © David Acosta Allely/Shutterstock.com, p. 14; © Miguel Schincariol/AFP/Getty Images, p. 15; © Jens Mommens/Shutterstock.com, p. 17; © SpazGenev/Shutterstock.com, pp. 18, 22, 23; © Abdul Razak Latif/Shutterstock.com, p. 24; © MrSegui/Shutterstock.com, p. 25; © Glen Berlin/Shutterstock.com, p. 27; © Art Konovalov/Shutterstock.com, p. 28; © Paul Popper/Popperfoto/Getty Images, p. 29 (top left); © Rolls Press/Popperfoto/Getty Images, p. 29 (top right); © Mike Hewitt/Allsport/Getty Images Sport/Getty Images, p. 29 (bottom left).

Front Cover: © Clive Mason/Getty Images Sport/Getty Images.